Off to School

by Michael Peters

PEARSON

Scott
Foresman

Editorial Offices: Glenview, Illinois • Parsippany, New Jersey • New York, New York
Sales Offices: Boston, Massachusetts • Duluth, Georgia • Glenview, Illinois
Coppell, Texas • Sacramento, California • Mesa, Arizona

I am on a bus.

I am in a car.

I am on a bike.

I am on a train.

I am on a skateboard.

I am on a scooter.

I am walking.